Emperor Penguins

Contents	Page

written by Rachel Walker

Penguins are so different from other birds that early explorers wondered if they were birds at all, or a different creature altogether. They walk standing upright like a person, rather than hopping along like a bird. They don't fly and they do swim.

Their feathers are waterproof and look like fish scales. These birds are a strange shape, with a large round body and much smaller head and feet, and short flat wings. Their strong black and white camouflage makes them look like men wearing suits!

The Emperor penguin is the largest species, similar in size to a chunky 10-year old person, making them the tallest and the heaviest penguin by far! The Emperor is much bigger than its cousin, the smaller King penguin, which has the same markings and follows a similar life cycle.

Even though Emperor penguins are such large birds, they aren't easy to find, because they are natives of Antarctica, the coldest place on Earth. Antarctica is a very remote part of the world, so only a few people ever visit there and see the Emperors in their own environment, near the South Pole.

Antarctica
SOUTH POLE
1898
1821
Scott 1902
80°
King Edward VII Land
Ice Barrier
SOUTH VICTORIA
Ross Sea
Mag. Pole (Ross)
Mag. Pole (Scott)
Adélie Land
Antarctic Circle
Scott I.
Balleny Is.

Unlike most birds,
penguins can't fly
in the air, but they
look as if they are
flying when they
swim! Their wings
have evolved into
flippers, which they
use like paddles,
making them superb
swimmers and divers.
Penguin's bodies are
a stream-lined shape,
and they have short
smooth feathers, so
they can glide quickly
and gracefully
through the icy water.
They are covered
with a thick layer of
blubber that traps
body heat, and their
overlapping feathers,
coated in oil, form a
waterproof layer to
keep them warm.

Penguins go to sea to hunt and eat. Emperor penguins are such good divers that they can hold their breath for 20 minutes and sometimes dive right to the ocean floor (far deeper than any other bird) as they catch fish, slippery squid, and tiny sea creatures named krill.

Emperors always dive and swim in groups, and although they
can hold their breath for a long, long time, most of their dives are
just six minutes long.

On land, most birds hop, but not the Emperor penguin, whose clumsy waddling on ice is very different from its graceful movement in the water. It alternates between walking and tobogganing over the slippery ice by sliding on its belly, propelled along by its feet and flat, firm flippers.

Emperors dive off the ice and into the sea. When they have finished hunting and feeding they use their powerful flippers to push themselves out of the water and back onto the ice.

Emperor penguins live in colonies of hundreds, where they follow an unusual life cycle:

- For the first 3 months every year they all feed in the ocean to build up their strength and develop a layer of blubber before the winter.
- In April the whole colony sets out on a tiring trek, marching inland for 60–100 miles further south.
- They reach their annual breeding ground and form pairs with their mates.

Unlike most birds – and even other types of penguins – Emperor
Penguins don't build nests and hatch their young in springtime.
Instead the female lays one egg on bare ice in May or June and
immediately puts it onto her mate's feet.

The male Emperor then tucks it under his brood pouch, which is a fold of feathery skin that keeps the egg warm while the chick develops. He begins the important job of protecting the egg through the coldest winter on Earth.

Emperor penguins can go for up to 120 days without any food, which is lucky because once the female has laid the egg and transferred it to the male's feet she goes to sea to hunt, leaving the male holding the egg. The female won't return for 62-66 days, so her mate has to take sole responsibility for the egg and can't leave it for a minute or it will freeze on the ice.

"Huddling" is a strange but necessary thing (that only Emperors do) to survive through the dark Antarctic winter. When icy winds blow and temperatures drop, hundreds of Emperors stand close together in groups or "huddles". They each take their turn shuffling – with their egg on their feet – to the outside of the group, to shelter others from the extreme cold.

When the female
does come back to
the colony in July
or August, it is still
dark in Antarctica
all day and all night,
so she has to call
out to find her mate.
Once the female
Emperor has found
him, their newly-
hatched chick is
carefully transferred
onto her feet and
tucked under her
brood pouch. Her
starving mate
immediately hurries
to the sea to fish for
3 weeks. When the
male returns from
fishing, both parents
will take turns
feeding regurgitated
seafood to their
baby chick.

20

By the time the chicks are 8 weeks old, the weather is warmer
and they are ready to leave their parents and huddle with the
other chicks in the colony. Both adult birds are free to go fishing
and come back regularly to feed their chicks for the first
4 or 5 months.

After that, the chicks are independent and soon learn to swim
and dive for their own food. If the Emperor chicks do survive
their first year of life in the coldest place on Earth, then they
will return to the same breeding colony year after year.